THIS BOOK BELONGS TO:

_____

_____

_____

Swatch Name .... Fabric Type .... Designer .... Content .... Colour .... Length .... Width .... Purchased From .... Cost Price .... ☐ Prewashed Used .... ☐ Used Up Care .... Notes	SWATCH

Swatch Name .... Fabric Type .... Designer .... Content .... Colour .... Length .... Width .... Purchased From .... Cost Price .... ☐ Prewashed Used .... ☐ Used Up Care .... Notes	SWATCH

Swatch Name .... Fabric Type .... Designer .... Content .... Colour .... Length .... Width .... Purchased From .... Cost Price .... ☐ Prewashed Used .... ☐ Used Up Care .... Notes	SWATCH

SWATCH	Swatch Name ....
	Fabric Type ....
	Designer ....
	Content .... Colour ....
	Length .... Width ....
	Purchased From ....
	Cost Price .... ☐ Prewashed
	Used ....
	.... ☐ Used Up
	Care ....
	Notes ....

SWATCH	Swatch Name ....
	Fabric Type ....
	Designer ....
	Content .... Colour ....
	Length .... Width ....
	Purchased From ....
	Cost Price .... ☐ Prewashed
	Used ....
	.... ☐ Used Up
	Care ....
	Notes ....

SWATCH	Swatch Name ....
	Fabric Type ....
	Designer ....
	Content .... Colour ....
	Length .... Width ....
	Purchased From ....
	Cost Price .... ☐ Prewashed
	Used ....
	.... ☐ Used Up
	Care ....
	Notes ....

Swatch Name .... Fabric Type .... Designer .... Content .... Colour .... Length .... Width .... Purchased From .... Cost Price .... ☐ Prewashed Used .... ☐ Used Up Care .... Notes	SWATCH

Swatch Name .... Fabric Type .... Designer .... Content .... Colour .... Length .... Width .... Purchased From .... Cost Price .... ☐ Prewashed Used .... ☐ Used Up Care .... Notes	SWATCH

Swatch Name .... Fabric Type .... Designer .... Content .... Colour .... Length .... Width .... Purchased From .... Cost Price .... ☐ Prewashed Used .... ☐ Used Up Care .... Notes	SWATCH

SWATCH

Swatch Name ....

Fabric Type ....

Designer ....

Content .... Colour ....

Length .... Width ....

Purchased From ....

Cost Price .... ☐ Prewashed

Used ....

.... ☐ Used Up

Care ....

Notes ....

SWATCH

Swatch Name ....

Fabric Type ....

Designer ....

Content .... Colour ....

Length .... Width ....

Purchased From ....

Cost Price .... ☐ Prewashed

Used ....

.... ☐ Used Up

Care ....

Notes ....

SWATCH

Swatch Name ....

Fabric Type ....

Designer ....

Content .... Colour ....

Length .... Width ....

Purchased From ....

Cost Price .... ☐ Prewashed

Used ....

.... ☐ Used Up

Care ....

Notes ....

Swatch Name .... Fabric Type .... Designer .... Content .... Colour .... Length .... Width .... Purchased From .... Cost Price .... ☐ Prewashed Used .... ☐ Used Up Care .... Notes	SWATCH

Swatch Name .... Fabric Type .... Designer .... Content .... Colour .... Length .... Width .... Purchased From .... Cost Price .... ☐ Prewashed Used .... ☐ Used Up Care .... Notes	SWATCH

Swatch Name .... Fabric Type .... Designer .... Content .... Colour .... Length .... Width .... Purchased From .... Cost Price .... ☐ Prewashed Used .... ☐ Used Up Care .... Notes	SWATCH

SWATCH

Swatch Name ....
Fabric Type ....
Designer ....
Content .... Colour ....
Length .... Width ....
Purchased From ....
Cost Price .... □ Prewashed
Used ....
.... □ Used Up
Care ....
Notes ....

SWATCH

Swatch Name ....
Fabric Type ....
Designer ....
Content .... Colour ....
Length .... Width ....
Purchased From ....
Cost Price .... □ Prewashed
Used ....
.... □ Used Up
Care ....
Notes ....

SWATCH

Swatch Name ....
Fabric Type ....
Designer ....
Content .... Colour ....
Length .... Width ....
Purchased From ....
Cost Price .... □ Prewashed
Used ....
.... □ Used Up
Care ....
Notes ....

Swatch Name ....

Fabric Type ....

Designer ....

Content .... Colour ....

Length .... Width ....

Purchased From ....

Cost Price .... ☐ Prewashed

Used ....

.... ☐ Used Up

Care ....

Notes ....

SWATCH

Swatch Name ....

Fabric Type ....

Designer ....

Content .... Colour ....

Length .... Width ....

Purchased From ....

Cost Price .... ☐ Prewashed

Used ....

.... ☐ Used Up

Care ....

Notes ....

SWATCH

Swatch Name ....

Fabric Type ....

Designer ....

Content .... Colour ....

Length .... Width ....

Purchased From ....

Cost Price .... ☐ Prewashed

Used ....

.... ☐ Used Up

Care ....

Notes ....

SWATCH

SWATCH	Swatch Name ....
	Fabric Type ....
	Designer ....
	Content .... Colour ....
	Length .... Width ....
	Purchased From ....
	Cost Price .... □ Prewashed
	Used ....
	.... □ Used Up
	Care ....
	Notes ....

SWATCH	Swatch Name ....
	Fabric Type ....
	Designer ....
	Content .... Colour ....
	Length .... Width ....
	Purchased From ....
	Cost Price .... □ Prewashed
	Used ....
	.... □ Used Up
	Care ....
	Notes ....

SWATCH	Swatch Name ....
	Fabric Type ....
	Designer ....
	Content .... Colour ....
	Length .... Width ....
	Purchased From ....
	Cost Price .... □ Prewashed
	Used ....
	.... □ Used Up
	Care ....
	Notes ....

Swatch Name ....

Fabric Type ....

Designer ....

Content .... Colour ....

Length .... Width ....

Purchased From ....

Cost Price .... □ Prewashed

Used ....

.... □ Used Up

Care ....

Notes ....

SWATCH

Swatch Name ....

Fabric Type ....

Designer ....

Content .... Colour ....

Length .... Width ....

Purchased From ....

Cost Price .... □ Prewashed

Used ....

.... □ Used Up

Care ....

Notes ....

SWATCH

Swatch Name ....

Fabric Type ....

Designer ....

Content .... Colour ....

Length .... Width ....

Purchased From ....

Cost Price .... □ Prewashed

Used ....

.... □ Used Up

Care ....

Notes ....

SWATCH

SWATCH

Swatch Name ....
Fabric Type ....
Designer ....
Content .... Colour ....
Length .... Width ....
Purchased From ....
Cost Price .... ☐ Prewashed
Used ....
.... ☐ Used Up
Care ....
Notes ....

SWATCH

Swatch Name ....
Fabric Type ....
Designer ....
Content .... Colour ....
Length .... Width ....
Purchased From ....
Cost Price .... ☐ Prewashed
Used ....
.... ☐ Used Up
Care ....
Notes ....

SWATCH

Swatch Name ....
Fabric Type ....
Designer ....
Content .... Colour ....
Length .... Width ....
Purchased From ....
Cost Price .... ☐ Prewashed
Used ....
.... ☐ Used Up
Care ....
Notes ....

Swatch Name	
Fabric Type	
Designer	
Content .... Colour	
Length .... Width	**SWATCH**
Purchased From	
Cost Price .... □ Prewashed	
Used	
.... □ Used Up	
Care	
Notes	

Swatch Name	
Fabric Type	
Designer	
Content .... Colour	
Length .... Width	**SWATCH**
Purchased From	
Cost Price .... □ Prewashed	
Used	
.... □ Used Up	
Care	
Notes	

Swatch Name	
Fabric Type	
Designer	
Content .... Colour	
Length .... Width	**SWATCH**
Purchased From	
Cost Price .... □ Prewashed	
Used	
.... □ Used Up	
Care	
Notes	

SWATCH	Swatch Name ....
	Fabric Type ....
	Designer ....
	Content .... Colour ....
	Length .... Width ....
	Purchased From ....
	Cost Price .... ☐ Prewashed
	Used ....
	.... ☐ Used Up
	Care ....
	Notes ....

SWATCH	Swatch Name ....
	Fabric Type ....
	Designer ....
	Content .... Colour ....
	Length .... Width ....
	Purchased From ....
	Cost Price .... ☐ Prewashed
	Used ....
	.... ☐ Used Up
	Care ....
	Notes ....

SWATCH	Swatch Name ....
	Fabric Type ....
	Designer ....
	Content .... Colour ....
	Length .... Width ....
	Purchased From ....
	Cost Price .... ☐ Prewashed
	Used ....
	.... ☐ Used Up
	Care ....
	Notes ....

Swatch Name ....

Fabric Type ....

Designer ....

Content .... Colour ....

Length .... Width ....

Purchased From ....

Cost Price .... ☐ Prewashed

Used ....

.... ☐ Used Up

Care ....

Notes ....

SWATCH

Swatch Name ....

Fabric Type ....

Designer ....

Content .... Colour ....

Length .... Width ....

Purchased From ....

Cost Price .... ☐ Prewashed

Used ....

.... ☐ Used Up

Care ....

Notes ....

SWATCH

Swatch Name ....

Fabric Type ....

Designer ....

Content .... Colour ....

Length .... Width ....

Purchased From ....

Cost Price .... ☐ Prewashed

Used ....

.... ☐ Used Up

Care ....

Notes ....

SWATCH

SWATCH

Swatch Name ....
Fabric Type ....
Designer ....
Content .... Colour ....
Length .... Width ....
Purchased From ....
Cost Price .... ☐ Prewashed
Used ....
.... ☐ Used Up
Care ....
Notes ....

SWATCH

Swatch Name ....
Fabric Type ....
Designer ....
Content .... Colour ....
Length .... Width ....
Purchased From ....
Cost Price .... ☐ Prewashed
Used ....
.... ☐ Used Up
Care ....
Notes ....

SWATCH

Swatch Name ....
Fabric Type ....
Designer ....
Content .... Colour ....
Length .... Width ....
Purchased From ....
Cost Price .... ☐ Prewashed
Used ....
.... ☐ Used Up
Care ....
Notes ....

Swatch Name ....

Fabric Type ....

Designer ....

Content .... Colour ....

Length .... Width ....

Purchased From ....

Cost Price .... □ Prewashed

Used ....

.... □ Used Up

Care ....

Notes ....

SWATCH

Swatch Name ....

Fabric Type ....

Designer ....

Content .... Colour ....

Length .... Width ....

Purchased From ....

Cost Price .... □ Prewashed

Used ....

.... □ Used Up

Care ....

Notes ....

SWATCH

Swatch Name ....

Fabric Type ....

Designer ....

Content .... Colour ....

Length .... Width ....

Purchased From ....

Cost Price .... □ Prewashed

Used ....

.... □ Used Up

Care ....

Notes ....

SWATCH

SWATCH

Swatch Name ....

Fabric Type ....

Designer ....

Content .... Colour ....

Length .... Width ....

Purchased From ....

Cost Price .... □ Prewashed

Used ....

.... □ Used Up

Care ....

Notes ....

SWATCH

Swatch Name ....

Fabric Type ....

Designer ....

Content .... Colour ....

Length .... Width ....

Purchased From ....

Cost Price .... □ Prewashed

Used ....

.... □ Used Up

Care ....

Notes ....

SWATCH

Swatch Name ....

Fabric Type ....

Designer ....

Content .... Colour ....

Length .... Width ....

Purchased From ....

Cost Price .... □ Prewashed

Used ....

.... □ Used Up

Care ....

Notes ....

Swatch Name ....
Fabric Type ....
Designer ....
Content .... Colour ....
Length .... Width ....
Purchased From ....
Cost Price .... ☐ Prewashed
Used ....
.... ☐ Used Up
Care ....
Notes ....

SWATCH

Swatch Name ....
Fabric Type ....
Designer ....
Content .... Colour ....
Length .... Width ....
Purchased From ....
Cost Price .... ☐ Prewashed
Used ....
.... ☐ Used Up
Care ....
Notes ....

SWATCH

Swatch Name ....
Fabric Type ....
Designer ....
Content .... Colour ....
Length .... Width ....
Purchased From ....
Cost Price .... ☐ Prewashed
Used ....
.... ☐ Used Up
Care ....
Notes ....

SWATCH

SWATCH

Swatch Name ....

Fabric Type ....

Designer ....

Content .... Colour ....

Length .... Width ....

Purchased From ....

Cost Price .... □ Prewashed

Used ....

.... □ Used Up

Care ....

Notes ....

SWATCH

Swatch Name ....

Fabric Type ....

Designer ....

Content .... Colour ....

Length .... Width ....

Purchased From ....

Cost Price .... □ Prewashed

Used ....

.... □ Used Up

Care ....

Notes ....

SWATCH

Swatch Name ....

Fabric Type ....

Designer ....

Content .... Colour ....

Length .... Width ....

Purchased From ....

Cost Price .... □ Prewashed

Used ....

.... □ Used Up

Care ....

Notes ....

Swatch Name ....
Fabric Type ....
Designer ....
Content .... Colour ....
Length .... Width ....
Purchased From ....
Cost Price .... □ Prewashed
Used ....
.... □ Used Up
Care ....
Notes ....

SWATCH

Swatch Name ....
Fabric Type ....
Designer ....
Content .... Colour ....
Length .... Width ....
Purchased From ....
Cost Price .... □ Prewashed
Used ....
.... □ Used Up
Care ....
Notes ....

SWATCH

Swatch Name ....
Fabric Type ....
Designer ....
Content .... Colour ....
Length .... Width ....
Purchased From ....
Cost Price .... □ Prewashed
Used ....
.... □ Used Up
Care ....
Notes ....

SWATCH

SWATCH	Swatch Name .... Fabric Type .... Designer .... Content .... Colour .... Length .... Width .... Purchased From .... Cost Price .... □ Prewashed Used .... □ Used Up Care .... Notes ....
SWATCH	Swatch Name .... Fabric Type .... Designer .... Content .... Colour .... Length .... Width .... Purchased From .... Cost Price .... □ Prewashed Used .... □ Used Up Care .... Notes ....
SWATCH	Swatch Name .... Fabric Type .... Designer .... Content .... Colour .... Length .... Width .... Purchased From .... Cost Price .... □ Prewashed Used .... □ Used Up Care .... Notes ....

Swatch Name ....

Fabric Type ....

Designer ....

Content .... Colour ....

Length .... Width ....

Purchased From ....

Cost Price .... □ Prewashed

Used ....

.... □ Used Up

Care ....

Notes ....

SWATCH

Swatch Name ....

Fabric Type ....

Designer ....

Content .... Colour ....

Length .... Width ....

Purchased From ....

Cost Price .... □ Prewashed

Used ....

.... □ Used Up

Care ....

Notes ....

SWATCH

Swatch Name ....

Fabric Type ....

Designer ....

Content .... Colour ....

Length .... Width ....

Purchased From ....

Cost Price .... □ Prewashed

Used ....

.... □ Used Up

Care ....

Notes ....

SWATCH

SWATCH	Swatch Name ....
	Fabric Type ....
	Designer ....
	Content .... Colour ....
	Length .... Width ....
	Purchased From ....
	Cost Price .... □ Prewashed
	Used ....
	.... □ Used Up
	Care ....
	Notes ....

SWATCH	Swatch Name ....
	Fabric Type ....
	Designer ....
	Content .... Colour ....
	Length .... Width ....
	Purchased From ....
	Cost Price .... □ Prewashed
	Used ....
	.... □ Used Up
	Care ....
	Notes ....

SWATCH	Swatch Name ....
	Fabric Type ....
	Designer ....
	Content .... Colour ....
	Length .... Width ....
	Purchased From ....
	Cost Price .... □ Prewashed
	Used ....
	.... □ Used Up
	Care ....
	Notes ....

Swatch Name ....

Fabric Type ....

Designer ....

Content .... Colour ....

Length .... Width ....

Purchased From ....

Cost Price .... □ Prewashed

Used ....

.... □ Used Up

Care ....

Notes ....

SWATCH

Swatch Name ....

Fabric Type ....

Designer ....

Content .... Colour ....

Length .... Width ....

Purchased From ....

Cost Price .... □ Prewashed

Used ....

.... □ Used Up

Care ....

Notes ....

SWATCH

Swatch Name ....

Fabric Type ....

Designer ....

Content .... Colour ....

Length .... Width ....

Purchased From ....

Cost Price .... □ Prewashed

Used ....

.... □ Used Up

Care ....

Notes ....

SWATCH

SWATCH

Swatch Name ....
Fabric Type ....
Designer ....
Content .... Colour ....
Length .... Width ....
Purchased From ....
Cost Price .... □ Prewashed
Used ....
.... □ Used Up
Care ....
Notes ....

SWATCH

Swatch Name ....
Fabric Type ....
Designer ....
Content .... Colour ....
Length .... Width ....
Purchased From ....
Cost Price .... □ Prewashed
Used ....
.... □ Used Up
Care ....
Notes ....

SWATCH

Swatch Name ....
Fabric Type ....
Designer ....
Content .... Colour ....
Length .... Width ....
Purchased From ....
Cost Price .... □ Prewashed
Used ....
.... □ Used Up
Care ....
Notes ....

Swatch Name ....

Fabric Type ....

Designer ....

Content .... Colour ....

Length .... Width ....

Purchased From ....

Cost Price .... □ Prewashed

Used ....

.... □ Used Up

Care ....

Notes ....

SWATCH

Swatch Name ....

Fabric Type ....

Designer ....

Content .... Colour ....

Length .... Width ....

Purchased From ....

Cost Price .... □ Prewashed

Used ....

.... □ Used Up

Care ....

Notes ....

SWATCH

Swatch Name ....

Fabric Type ....

Designer ....

Content .... Colour ....

Length .... Width ....

Purchased From ....

Cost Price .... □ Prewashed

Used ....

.... □ Used Up

Care ....

Notes ....

SWATCH

SWATCH

Swatch Name ....
Fabric Type ....
Designer ....
Content .... Colour ....
Length .... Width ....
Purchased From ....
Cost Price .... □ Prewashed
Used ....
.... □ Used Up
Care ....
Notes ....

SWATCH

Swatch Name ....
Fabric Type ....
Designer ....
Content .... Colour ....
Length .... Width ....
Purchased From ....
Cost Price .... □ Prewashed
Used ....
.... □ Used Up
Care ....
Notes ....

SWATCH

Swatch Name ....
Fabric Type ....
Designer ....
Content .... Colour ....
Length .... Width ....
Purchased From ....
Cost Price .... □ Prewashed
Used ....
.... □ Used Up
Care ....
Notes ....

Swatch Name ....

Fabric Type ....

Designer ....

Content .... Colour ....

Length .... Width ....

Purchased From ....

Cost Price .... ☐ Prewashed

Used ....

.... ☐ Used Up

Care ....

Notes ....

SWATCH

Swatch Name ....

Fabric Type ....

Designer ....

Content .... Colour ....

Length .... Width ....

Purchased From ....

Cost Price .... ☐ Prewashed

Used ....

.... ☐ Used Up

Care ....

Notes ....

SWATCH

Swatch Name ....

Fabric Type ....

Designer ....

Content .... Colour ....

Length .... Width ....

Purchased From ....

Cost Price .... ☐ Prewashed

Used ....

.... ☐ Used Up

Care ....

Notes ....

SWATCH

SWATCH

Swatch Name ....

Fabric Type ....

Designer ....

Content .... Colour ....

Length .... Width ....

Purchased From ....

Cost Price .... □ Prewashed

Used ....

.... □ Used Up

Care ....

Notes ....

SWATCH

Swatch Name ....

Fabric Type ....

Designer ....

Content .... Colour ....

Length .... Width ....

Purchased From ....

Cost Price .... □ Prewashed

Used ....

.... □ Used Up

Care ....

Notes ....

SWATCH

Swatch Name ....

Fabric Type ....

Designer ....

Content .... Colour ....

Length .... Width ....

Purchased From ....

Cost Price .... □ Prewashed

Used ....

.... □ Used Up

Care ....

Notes ....

Swatch Name	
Fabric Type	
Designer	
Content .... Colour	SWATCH
Length .... Width	
Purchased From	
Cost Price .... ☐ Prewashed	
Used	
.... ☐ Used Up	
Care	
Notes	

Swatch Name	
Fabric Type	
Designer	
Content .... Colour	SWATCH
Length .... Width	
Purchased From	
Cost Price .... ☐ Prewashed	
Used	
.... ☐ Used Up	
Care	
Notes	

Swatch Name	
Fabric Type	
Designer	
Content .... Colour	SWATCH
Length .... Width	
Purchased From	
Cost Price .... ☐ Prewashed	
Used	
.... ☐ Used Up	
Care	
Notes	

SWATCH

Swatch Name ....
Fabric Type ....
Designer ....
Content .... Colour ....
Length .... Width ....
Purchased From ....
Cost Price .... □ Prewashed
Used ....
.... □ Used Up
Care ....
Notes ....

SWATCH

Swatch Name ....
Fabric Type ....
Designer ....
Content .... Colour ....
Length .... Width ....
Purchased From ....
Cost Price .... □ Prewashed
Used ....
.... □ Used Up
Care ....
Notes ....

SWATCH

Swatch Name ....
Fabric Type ....
Designer ....
Content .... Colour ....
Length .... Width ....
Purchased From ....
Cost Price .... □ Prewashed
Used ....
.... □ Used Up
Care ....
Notes ....

Swatch Name	
Fabric Type	SWATCH
Designer	
Content .... Colour	
Length .... Width	
Purchased From	
Cost Price .... ☐ Prewashed	
Used	
.... ☐ Used Up	
Care	
Notes	

Swatch Name	
Fabric Type	SWATCH
Designer	
Content .... Colour	
Length .... Width	
Purchased From	
Cost Price .... ☐ Prewashed	
Used	
.... ☐ Used Up	
Care	
Notes	

Swatch Name	
Fabric Type	SWATCH
Designer	
Content .... Colour	
Length .... Width	
Purchased From	
Cost Price .... ☐ Prewashed	
Used	
.... ☐ Used Up	
Care	
Notes	

SWATCH

Swatch Name ....
Fabric Type ....
Designer ....
Content .... Colour ....
Length .... Width ....
Purchased From ....
Cost Price .... □ Prewashed
Used ....
.... □ Used Up
Care ....
Notes ....

SWATCH

Swatch Name ....
Fabric Type ....
Designer ....
Content .... Colour ....
Length .... Width ....
Purchased From ....
Cost Price .... □ Prewashed
Used ....
.... □ Used Up
Care ....
Notes ....

SWATCH

Swatch Name ....
Fabric Type ....
Designer ....
Content .... Colour ....
Length .... Width ....
Purchased From ....
Cost Price .... □ Prewashed
Used ....
.... □ Used Up
Care ....
Notes ....

Swatch Name	
Fabric Type	
Designer	
Content .... Colour	
Length .... Width	**SWATCH**
Purchased From	
Cost Price .... ☐ Prewashed	
Used	
.... ☐ Used Up	
Care	
Notes	

Swatch Name	
Fabric Type	
Designer	
Content .... Colour	
Length .... Width	**SWATCH**
Purchased From	
Cost Price .... ☐ Prewashed	
Used	
.... ☐ Used Up	
Care	
Notes	

Swatch Name	
Fabric Type	
Designer	
Content .... Colour	
Length .... Width	**SWATCH**
Purchased From	
Cost Price .... ☐ Prewashed	
Used	
.... ☐ Used Up	
Care	
Notes	

SWATCH

Swatch Name ....
Fabric Type ....
Designer ....
Content .... Colour ....
Length .... Width ....
Purchased From ....
Cost Price .... ☐ Prewashed
Used ....
.... ☐ Used Up
Care ....
Notes ....

SWATCH

Swatch Name ....
Fabric Type ....
Designer ....
Content .... Colour ....
Length .... Width ....
Purchased From ....
Cost Price .... ☐ Prewashed
Used ....
.... ☐ Used Up
Care ....
Notes ....

SWATCH

Swatch Name ....
Fabric Type ....
Designer ....
Content .... Colour ....
Length .... Width ....
Purchased From ....
Cost Price .... ☐ Prewashed
Used ....
.... ☐ Used Up
Care ....
Notes ....

Swatch Name ....
Fabric Type ....
Designer ....
Content .... Colour ....
Length .... Width ....
Purchased From ....
Cost Price .... ☐ Prewashed
Used ....
.... ☐ Used Up
Care ....
Notes ....

SWATCH

Swatch Name ....
Fabric Type ....
Designer ....
Content .... Colour ....
Length .... Width ....
Purchased From ....
Cost Price .... ☐ Prewashed
Used ....
.... ☐ Used Up
Care ....
Notes ....

SWATCH

Swatch Name ....
Fabric Type ....
Designer ....
Content .... Colour ....
Length .... Width ....
Purchased From ....
Cost Price .... ☐ Prewashed
Used ....
.... ☐ Used Up
Care ....
Notes ....

SWATCH

SWATCH

Swatch Name ....

Fabric Type ....

Designer ....

Content .... Colour ....

Length .... Width ....

Purchased From ....

Cost Price .... ☐ Prewashed

Used ....

.... ☐ Used Up

Care ....

Notes ....

SWATCH

Swatch Name ....

Fabric Type ....

Designer ....

Content .... Colour ....

Length .... Width ....

Purchased From ....

Cost Price .... ☐ Prewashed

Used ....

.... ☐ Used Up

Care ....

Notes ....

SWATCH

Swatch Name ....

Fabric Type ....

Designer ....

Content .... Colour ....

Length .... Width ....

Purchased From ....

Cost Price .... ☐ Prewashed

Used ....

.... ☐ Used Up

Care ....

Notes ....

Swatch Name ....
Fabric Type ....
Designer ....
Content .... Colour ....
Length .... Width ....
Purchased From ....
Cost Price .... ☐ Prewashed
Used ....
.... ☐ Used Up
Care ....
Notes ....

SWATCH

Swatch Name ....
Fabric Type ....
Designer ....
Content .... Colour ....
Length .... Width ....
Purchased From ....
Cost Price .... ☐ Prewashed
Used ....
.... ☐ Used Up
Care ....
Notes ....

SWATCH

Swatch Name ....
Fabric Type ....
Designer ....
Content .... Colour ....
Length .... Width ....
Purchased From ....
Cost Price .... ☐ Prewashed
Used ....
.... ☐ Used Up
Care ....
Notes ....

SWATCH

SWATCH

Swatch Name ....
Fabric Type ....
Designer ....
Content .... Colour ....
Length .... Width ....
Purchased From ....
Cost Price .... □ Prewashed
Used ....
.... □ Used Up
Care ....
Notes ....

SWATCH

Swatch Name ....
Fabric Type ....
Designer ....
Content .... Colour ....
Length .... Width ....
Purchased From ....
Cost Price .... □ Prewashed
Used ....
.... □ Used Up
Care ....
Notes ....

SWATCH

Swatch Name ....
Fabric Type ....
Designer ....
Content .... Colour ....
Length .... Width ....
Purchased From ....
Cost Price .... □ Prewashed
Used ....
.... □ Used Up
Care ....
Notes ....

Swatch Name ....

Fabric Type ....

Designer ....

Content .... Colour ....

Length .... Width ....

Purchased From ....

Cost Price .... □ Prewashed

Used ....

.... □ Used Up

Care ....

Notes ....

SWATCH

Swatch Name ....

Fabric Type ....

Designer ....

Content .... Colour ....

Length .... Width ....

Purchased From ....

Cost Price .... □ Prewashed

Used ....

.... □ Used Up

Care ....

Notes ....

SWATCH

Swatch Name ....

Fabric Type ....

Designer ....

Content .... Colour ....

Length .... Width ....

Purchased From ....

Cost Price .... □ Prewashed

Used ....

.... □ Used Up

Care ....

Notes ....

SWATCH

SWATCH

Swatch Name ....

Fabric Type ....

Designer ....

Content .... Colour ....

Length .... Width ....

Purchased From ....

Cost Price .... □ Prewashed

Used ....

.... □ Used Up

Care ....

Notes ....

SWATCH

Swatch Name ....

Fabric Type ....

Designer ....

Content .... Colour ....

Length .... Width ....

Purchased From ....

Cost Price .... □ Prewashed

Used ....

.... □ Used Up

Care ....

Notes ....

SWATCH

Swatch Name ....

Fabric Type ....

Designer ....

Content .... Colour ....

Length .... Width ....

Purchased From ....

Cost Price .... □ Prewashed

Used ....

.... □ Used Up

Care ....

Notes ....

Swatch Name ....

Fabric Type ....

Designer ....

Content .... Colour ....

Length .... Width ....

Purchased From ....

Cost Price .... □ Prewashed

Used ....

.... □ Used Up

Care ....

Notes ....

SWATCH

Swatch Name ....

Fabric Type ....

Designer ....

Content .... Colour ....

Length .... Width ....

Purchased From ....

Cost Price .... □ Prewashed

Used ....

.... □ Used Up

Care ....

Notes ....

SWATCH

Swatch Name ....

Fabric Type ....

Designer ....

Content .... Colour ....

Length .... Width ....

Purchased From ....

Cost Price .... □ Prewashed

Used ....

.... □ Used Up

Care ....

Notes ....

SWATCH

SWATCH

Swatch Name ....
Fabric Type ....
Designer ....
Content .... Colour ....
Length .... Width ....
Purchased From ....
Cost Price .... ☐ Prewashed
Used ....
.... ☐ Used Up
Care ....
Notes ....

SWATCH

Swatch Name ....
Fabric Type ....
Designer ....
Content .... Colour ....
Length .... Width ....
Purchased From ....
Cost Price .... ☐ Prewashed
Used ....
.... ☐ Used Up
Care ....
Notes ....

SWATCH

Swatch Name ....
Fabric Type ....
Designer ....
Content .... Colour ....
Length .... Width ....
Purchased From ....
Cost Price .... ☐ Prewashed
Used ....
.... ☐ Used Up
Care ....
Notes ....

Swatch Name ....
Fabric Type ....
Designer ....
Content .... Colour ....
Length .... Width ....
Purchased From ....
Cost Price .... □ Prewashed
Used ....
.... □ Used Up
Care ....
Notes ....

SWATCH

Swatch Name ....
Fabric Type ....
Designer ....
Content .... Colour ....
Length .... Width ....
Purchased From ....
Cost Price .... □ Prewashed
Used ....
.... □ Used Up
Care ....
Notes ....

SWATCH

Swatch Name ....
Fabric Type ....
Designer ....
Content .... Colour ....
Length .... Width ....
Purchased From ....
Cost Price .... □ Prewashed
Used ....
.... □ Used Up
Care ....
Notes ....

SWATCH

SWATCH

Swatch Name ....

Fabric Type ....

Designer ....

Content .... Colour ....

Length .... Width ....

Purchased From ....

Cost Price .... ☐ Prewashed

Used ....

.... ☐ Used Up

Care ....

Notes ....

SWATCH

Swatch Name ....

Fabric Type ....

Designer ....

Content .... Colour ....

Length .... Width ....

Purchased From ....

Cost Price .... ☐ Prewashed

Used ....

.... ☐ Used Up

Care ....

Notes ....

SWATCH

Swatch Name ....

Fabric Type ....

Designer ....

Content .... Colour ....

Length .... Width ....

Purchased From ....

Cost Price .... ☐ Prewashed

Used ....

.... ☐ Used Up

Care ....

Notes ....

Swatch Name	
Fabric Type	
Designer	
Content	Colour
Length	Width
Purchased From	
Cost Price	☐ Prewashed
Used	
	☐ Used Up
Care	
Notes	

SWATCH

Swatch Name	
Fabric Type	
Designer	
Content	Colour
Length	Width
Purchased From	
Cost Price	☐ Prewashed
Used	
	☐ Used Up
Care	
Notes	

SWATCH

Swatch Name	
Fabric Type	
Designer	
Content	Colour
Length	Width
Purchased From	
Cost Price	☐ Prewashed
Used	
	☐ Used Up
Care	
Notes	

SWATCH

SWATCH

Swatch Name ....
Fabric Type ....
Designer ....
Content .... Colour ....
Length .... Width ....
Purchased From ....
Cost Price .... □ Prewashed
Used ....
.... □ Used Up
Care ....
Notes ....

SWATCH

Swatch Name ....
Fabric Type ....
Designer ....
Content .... Colour ....
Length .... Width ....
Purchased From ....
Cost Price .... □ Prewashed
Used ....
.... □ Used Up
Care ....
Notes ....

SWATCH

Swatch Name ....
Fabric Type ....
Designer ....
Content .... Colour ....
Length .... Width ....
Purchased From ....
Cost Price .... □ Prewashed
Used ....
.... □ Used Up
Care ....
Notes ....

Swatch Name ....

Fabric Type ....

Designer ....

Content .... Colour ....

Length .... Width ....

Purchased From ....

Cost Price .... ☐ Prewashed

Used ....

.... ☐ Used Up

Care ....

Notes ....

SWATCH

Swatch Name ....

Fabric Type ....

Designer ....

Content .... Colour ....

Length .... Width ....

Purchased From ....

Cost Price .... ☐ Prewashed

Used ....

.... ☐ Used Up

Care ....

Notes ....

SWATCH

Swatch Name ....

Fabric Type ....

Designer ....

Content .... Colour ....

Length .... Width ....

Purchased From ....

Cost Price .... ☐ Prewashed

Used ....

.... ☐ Used Up

Care ....

Notes ....

SWATCH

SWATCH

Swatch Name ....
Fabric Type ....
Designer ....
Content .... Colour ....
Length .... Width ....
Purchased From ....
Cost Price .... □ Prewashed
Used ....
.... □ Used Up
Care ....
Notes ....

SWATCH

Swatch Name ....
Fabric Type ....
Designer ....
Content .... Colour ....
Length .... Width ....
Purchased From ....
Cost Price .... □ Prewashed
Used ....
.... □ Used Up
Care ....
Notes ....

SWATCH

Swatch Name ....
Fabric Type ....
Designer ....
Content .... Colour ....
Length .... Width ....
Purchased From ....
Cost Price .... □ Prewashed
Used ....
.... □ Used Up
Care ....
Notes ....

Swatch Name ....
Fabric Type ....
Designer ....
Content .... Colour ....
Length .... Width ....
Purchased From ....
Cost Price .... ☐ Prewashed
Used ....
.... ☐ Used Up
Care ....
Notes ....

SWATCH

Swatch Name ....
Fabric Type ....
Designer ....
Content .... Colour ....
Length .... Width ....
Purchased From ....
Cost Price .... ☐ Prewashed
Used ....
.... ☐ Used Up
Care ....
Notes ....

SWATCH

Swatch Name ....
Fabric Type ....
Designer ....
Content .... Colour ....
Length .... Width ....
Purchased From ....
Cost Price .... ☐ Prewashed
Used ....
.... ☐ Used Up
Care ....
Notes ....

SWATCH

SWATCH

Swatch Name ....

Fabric Type ....

Designer ....

Content .... Colour ....

Length .... Width ....

Purchased From ....

Cost Price .... ☐ Prewashed

Used ....

.... ☐ Used Up

Care ....

Notes ....

SWATCH

Swatch Name ....

Fabric Type ....

Designer ....

Content .... Colour ....

Length .... Width ....

Purchased From ....

Cost Price .... ☐ Prewashed

Used ....

.... ☐ Used Up

Care ....

Notes ....

SWATCH

Swatch Name ....

Fabric Type ....

Designer ....

Content .... Colour ....

Length .... Width ....

Purchased From ....

Cost Price .... ☐ Prewashed

Used ....

.... ☐ Used Up

Care ....

Notes ....

Swatch Name ....
Fabric Type ....
Designer ....
Content .... Colour ....
Length .... Width ....
Purchased From ....
Cost Price .... □ Prewashed
Used ....
.... □ Used Up
Care ....
Notes ....

SWATCH

Swatch Name ....
Fabric Type ....
Designer ....
Content .... Colour ....
Length .... Width ....
Purchased From ....
Cost Price .... □ Prewashed
Used ....
.... □ Used Up
Care ....
Notes ....

SWATCH

Swatch Name ....
Fabric Type ....
Designer ....
Content .... Colour ....
Length .... Width ....
Purchased From ....
Cost Price .... □ Prewashed
Used ....
.... □ Used Up
Care ....
Notes ....

SWATCH

SWATCH	Swatch Name ....
	Fabric Type ....
	Designer ....
	Content .... Colour ....
	Length .... Width ....
	Purchased From ....
	Cost Price .... □ Prewashed
	Used ....
	.... □ Used Up
	Care ....
	Notes ....

SWATCH	Swatch Name ....
	Fabric Type ....
	Designer ....
	Content .... Colour ....
	Length .... Width ....
	Purchased From ....
	Cost Price .... □ Prewashed
	Used ....
	.... □ Used Up
	Care ....
	Notes ....

SWATCH	Swatch Name ....
	Fabric Type ....
	Designer ....
	Content .... Colour ....
	Length .... Width ....
	Purchased From ....
	Cost Price .... □ Prewashed
	Used ....
	.... □ Used Up
	Care ....
	Notes ....

Swatch Name ....

Fabric Type ....

Designer ....

Content .... Colour ....

Length .... Width ....

Purchased From ....

Cost Price .... ☐ Prewashed

Used ....

.... ☐ Used Up

Care ....

Notes ....

SWATCH

Swatch Name ....

Fabric Type ....

Designer ....

Content .... Colour ....

Length .... Width ....

Purchased From ....

Cost Price .... ☐ Prewashed

Used ....

.... ☐ Used Up

Care ....

Notes ....

SWATCH

Swatch Name ....

Fabric Type ....

Designer ....

Content .... Colour ....

Length .... Width ....

Purchased From ....

Cost Price .... ☐ Prewashed

Used ....

.... ☐ Used Up

Care ....

Notes ....

SWATCH

SWATCH

Swatch Name ....
Fabric Type ....
Designer ....
Content .... Colour ....
Length .... Width ....
Purchased From ....
Cost Price .... □ Prewashed
Used ....
.... □ Used Up
Care ....
Notes ....

SWATCH

Swatch Name ....
Fabric Type ....
Designer ....
Content .... Colour ....
Length .... Width ....
Purchased From ....
Cost Price .... □ Prewashed
Used ....
.... □ Used Up
Care ....
Notes ....

SWATCH

Swatch Name ....
Fabric Type ....
Designer ....
Content .... Colour ....
Length .... Width ....
Purchased From ....
Cost Price .... □ Prewashed
Used ....
.... □ Used Up
Care ....
Notes ....

Swatch Name .... Fabric Type .... Designer .... Content .... Colour .... Length .... Width .... Purchased From .... Cost Price .... ☐ Prewashed Used .... ☐ Used Up Care .... Notes	SWATCH

Swatch Name .... Fabric Type .... Designer .... Content .... Colour .... Length .... Width .... Purchased From .... Cost Price .... ☐ Prewashed Used .... ☐ Used Up Care .... Notes	SWATCH

Swatch Name .... Fabric Type .... Designer .... Content .... Colour .... Length .... Width .... Purchased From .... Cost Price .... ☐ Prewashed Used .... ☐ Used Up Care .... Notes	SWATCH

SWATCH

Swatch Name ....
Fabric Type ....
Designer ....
Content .... Colour ....
Length .... Width ....
Purchased From ....
Cost Price .... ☐ Prewashed
Used ....
.... ☐ Used Up
Care ....
Notes ....

SWATCH

Swatch Name ....
Fabric Type ....
Designer ....
Content .... Colour ....
Length .... Width ....
Purchased From ....
Cost Price .... ☐ Prewashed
Used ....
.... ☐ Used Up
Care ....
Notes ....

SWATCH

Swatch Name ....
Fabric Type ....
Designer ....
Content .... Colour ....
Length .... Width ....
Purchased From ....
Cost Price .... ☐ Prewashed
Used ....
.... ☐ Used Up
Care ....
Notes ....

Swatch Name ....

Fabric Type ....

Designer ....

Content .... Colour ....

Length .... Width ....

Purchased From ....

Cost Price .... ☐ Prewashed

Used ....

.... ☐ Used Up

Care ....

Notes ....

SWATCH

Swatch Name ....

Fabric Type ....

Designer ....

Content .... Colour ....

Length .... Width ....

Purchased From ....

Cost Price .... ☐ Prewashed

Used ....

.... ☐ Used Up

Care ....

Notes ....

SWATCH

Swatch Name ....

Fabric Type ....

Designer ....

Content .... Colour ....

Length .... Width ....

Purchased From ....

Cost Price .... ☐ Prewashed

Used ....

.... ☐ Used Up

Care ....

Notes ....

SWATCH

SWATCH

Swatch Name ....
Fabric Type ....
Designer ....
Content .... Colour ....
Length .... Width ....
Purchased From ....
Cost Price .... □ Prewashed
Used ....
.... □ Used Up
Care ....
Notes ....

SWATCH

Swatch Name ....
Fabric Type ....
Designer ....
Content .... Colour ....
Length .... Width ....
Purchased From ....
Cost Price .... □ Prewashed
Used ....
.... □ Used Up
Care ....
Notes ....

SWATCH

Swatch Name ....
Fabric Type ....
Designer ....
Content .... Colour ....
Length .... Width ....
Purchased From ....
Cost Price .... □ Prewashed
Used ....
.... □ Used Up
Care ....
Notes ....

Swatch Name ....

Fabric Type ....

Designer ....

Content .... Colour ....

Length .... Width ....

Purchased From ....

Cost Price .... □ Prewashed

Used ....

.... □ Used Up

Care ....

Notes ....

SWATCH

Swatch Name ....

Fabric Type ....

Designer ....

Content .... Colour ....

Length .... Width ....

Purchased From ....

Cost Price .... □ Prewashed

Used ....

.... □ Used Up

Care ....

Notes ....

SWATCH

Swatch Name ....

Fabric Type ....

Designer ....

Content .... Colour ....

Length .... Width ....

Purchased From ....

Cost Price .... □ Prewashed

Used ....

.... □ Used Up

Care ....

Notes ....

SWATCH

SWATCH	Swatch Name ....
	Fabric Type ....
	Designer ....
	Content .... Colour ....
	Length .... Width ....
	Purchased From ....
	Cost Price .... □ Prewashed
	Used ....
	.... □ Used Up
	Care ....
	Notes ....

SWATCH	Swatch Name ....
	Fabric Type ....
	Designer ....
	Content .... Colour ....
	Length .... Width ....
	Purchased From ....
	Cost Price .... □ Prewashed
	Used ....
	.... □ Used Up
	Care ....
	Notes ....

SWATCH	Swatch Name ....
	Fabric Type ....
	Designer ....
	Content .... Colour ....
	Length .... Width ....
	Purchased From ....
	Cost Price .... □ Prewashed
	Used ....
	.... □ Used Up
	Care ....
	Notes ....

Swatch Name ....

Fabric Type ....

Designer ....

Content .... Colour ....

Length .... Width ....

Purchased From ....

Cost Price .... □ Prewashed

Used ....

.... □ Used Up

Care ....

Notes ....

SWATCH

Swatch Name ....

Fabric Type ....

Designer ....

Content .... Colour ....

Length .... Width ....

Purchased From ....

Cost Price .... □ Prewashed

Used ....

.... □ Used Up

Care ....

Notes ....

SWATCH

Swatch Name ....

Fabric Type ....

Designer ....

Content .... Colour ....

Length .... Width ....

Purchased From ....

Cost Price .... □ Prewashed

Used ....

.... □ Used Up

Care ....

Notes ....

SWATCH

SWATCH

Swatch Name ....

Fabric Type ....

Designer ....

Content .... Colour ....

Length .... Width ....

Purchased From ....

Cost Price .... □ Prewashed

Used ....

.... □ Used Up

Care ....

Notes ....

SWATCH

Swatch Name ....

Fabric Type ....

Designer ....

Content .... Colour ....

Length .... Width ....

Purchased From ....

Cost Price .... □ Prewashed

Used ....

.... □ Used Up

Care ....

Notes ....

SWATCH

Swatch Name ....

Fabric Type ....

Designer ....

Content .... Colour ....

Length .... Width ....

Purchased From ....

Cost Price .... □ Prewashed

Used ....

.... □ Used Up

Care ....

Notes ....

Swatch Name ....

Fabric Type ....

Designer ....

Content .... Colour ....

Length .... Width ....

Purchased From ....

Cost Price .... □ Prewashed

Used ....

.... □ Used Up

Care ....

Notes ....

SWATCH

Swatch Name ....

Fabric Type ....

Designer ....

Content .... Colour ....

Length .... Width ....

Purchased From ....

Cost Price .... □ Prewashed

Used ....

.... □ Used Up

Care ....

Notes ....

SWATCH

Swatch Name ....

Fabric Type ....

Designer ....

Content .... Colour ....

Length .... Width ....

Purchased From ....

Cost Price .... □ Prewashed

Used ....

.... □ Used Up

Care ....

Notes ....

SWATCH

SWATCH

Swatch Name ....
Fabric Type ....
Designer ....
Content .... Colour ....
Length .... Width ....
Purchased From ....
Cost Price .... ☐ Prewashed
Used ....
.... ☐ Used Up
Care ....
Notes ....

SWATCH

Swatch Name ....
Fabric Type ....
Designer ....
Content .... Colour ....
Length .... Width ....
Purchased From ....
Cost Price .... ☐ Prewashed
Used ....
.... ☐ Used Up
Care ....
Notes ....

SWATCH

Swatch Name ....
Fabric Type ....
Designer ....
Content .... Colour ....
Length .... Width ....
Purchased From ....
Cost Price .... ☐ Prewashed
Used ....
.... ☐ Used Up
Care ....
Notes ....

Swatch Name ....

Fabric Type ....

Designer ....

Content .... Colour ....

Length .... Width ....

Purchased From ....

Cost Price .... ☐ Prewashed

Used ....

.... ☐ Used Up

Care ....

Notes ....

SWATCH

Swatch Name ....

Fabric Type ....

Designer ....

Content .... Colour ....

Length .... Width ....

Purchased From ....

Cost Price .... ☐ Prewashed

Used ....

.... ☐ Used Up

Care ....

Notes ....

SWATCH

Swatch Name ....

Fabric Type ....

Designer ....

Content .... Colour ....

Length .... Width ....

Purchased From ....

Cost Price .... ☐ Prewashed

Used ....

.... ☐ Used Up

Care ....

Notes ....

SWATCH

SWATCH	Swatch Name .... Fabric Type .... Designer .... Content .... Colour .... Length .... Width .... Purchased From .... Cost Price .... □ Prewashed Used .... □ Used Up Care .... Notes ....

SWATCH	Swatch Name .... Fabric Type .... Designer .... Content .... Colour .... Length .... Width .... Purchased From .... Cost Price .... □ Prewashed Used .... □ Used Up Care .... Notes ....

SWATCH	Swatch Name .... Fabric Type .... Designer .... Content .... Colour .... Length .... Width .... Purchased From .... Cost Price .... □ Prewashed Used .... □ Used Up Care .... Notes ....

Swatch Name ....

Fabric Type ....

Designer ....

Content .... Colour ....

Length .... Width ....

Purchased From ....

Cost Price .... □ Prewashed

Used ....

.... □ Used Up

Care ....

Notes ....

SWATCH

Swatch Name ....

Fabric Type ....

Designer ....

Content .... Colour ....

Length .... Width ....

Purchased From ....

Cost Price .... □ Prewashed

Used ....

.... □ Used Up

Care ....

Notes ....

SWATCH

Swatch Name ....

Fabric Type ....

Designer ....

Content .... Colour ....

Length .... Width ....

Purchased From ....

Cost Price .... □ Prewashed

Used ....

.... □ Used Up

Care ....

Notes ....

SWATCH

SWATCH

Swatch Name ....
Fabric Type ....
Designer ....
Content .... Colour ....
Length .... Width ....
Purchased From ....
Cost Price .... ☐ Prewashed
Used ....
.... ☐ Used Up
Care ....
Notes ....

SWATCH

Swatch Name ....
Fabric Type ....
Designer ....
Content .... Colour ....
Length .... Width ....
Purchased From ....
Cost Price .... ☐ Prewashed
Used ....
.... ☐ Used Up
Care ....
Notes ....

SWATCH

Swatch Name ....
Fabric Type ....
Designer ....
Content .... Colour ....
Length .... Width ....
Purchased From ....
Cost Price .... ☐ Prewashed
Used ....
.... ☐ Used Up
Care ....
Notes ....

Swatch Name ....

Fabric Type ....

Designer ....

Content .... Colour ....

Length .... Width ....

Purchased From ....

Cost Price .... □ Prewashed

Used ....

.... □ Used Up

Care ....

Notes ....

SWATCH

Swatch Name ....

Fabric Type ....

Designer ....

Content .... Colour ....

Length .... Width ....

Purchased From ....

Cost Price .... □ Prewashed

Used ....

.... □ Used Up

Care ....

Notes ....

SWATCH

Swatch Name ....

Fabric Type ....

Designer ....

Content .... Colour ....

Length .... Width ....

Purchased From ....

Cost Price .... □ Prewashed

Used ....

.... □ Used Up

Care ....

Notes ....

SWATCH

SWATCH

Swatch Name ....
Fabric Type ....
Designer ....
Content .... Colour ....
Length .... Width ....
Purchased From ....
Cost Price .... ☐ Prewashed
Used ....
.... ☐ Used Up
Care ....
Notes ....

SWATCH

Swatch Name ....
Fabric Type ....
Designer ....
Content .... Colour ....
Length .... Width ....
Purchased From ....
Cost Price .... ☐ Prewashed
Used ....
.... ☐ Used Up
Care ....
Notes ....

SWATCH

Swatch Name ....
Fabric Type ....
Designer ....
Content .... Colour ....
Length .... Width ....
Purchased From ....
Cost Price .... ☐ Prewashed
Used ....
.... ☐ Used Up
Care ....
Notes ....

Swatch Name ....

Fabric Type ....

Designer ....

Content .... Colour ....

Length .... Width ....

Purchased From ....

Cost Price .... ☐ Prewashed

Used ....

.... ☐ Used Up

Care ....

Notes ....

SWATCH

Swatch Name ....

Fabric Type ....

Designer ....

Content .... Colour ....

Length .... Width ....

Purchased From ....

Cost Price .... ☐ Prewashed

Used ....

.... ☐ Used Up

Care ....

Notes ....

SWATCH

Swatch Name ....

Fabric Type ....

Designer ....

Content .... Colour ....

Length .... Width ....

Purchased From ....

Cost Price .... ☐ Prewashed

Used ....

.... ☐ Used Up

Care ....

Notes ....

SWATCH

SWATCH

Swatch Name ....

Fabric Type ....

Designer ....

Content .... Colour ....

Length .... Width ....

Purchased From ....

Cost Price .... □ Prewashed

Used ....

.... □ Used Up

Care ....

Notes ....

SWATCH

Swatch Name ....

Fabric Type ....

Designer ....

Content .... Colour ....

Length .... Width ....

Purchased From ....

Cost Price .... □ Prewashed

Used ....

.... □ Used Up

Care ....

Notes ....

SWATCH

Swatch Name ....

Fabric Type ....

Designer ....

Content .... Colour ....

Length .... Width ....

Purchased From ....

Cost Price .... □ Prewashed

Used ....

.... □ Used Up

Care ....

Notes ....

Swatch Name ....

Fabric Type ....

Designer ....

Content .... Colour ....

Length .... Width ....

Purchased From ....

Cost Price .... ☐ Prewashed

Used ....

.... ☐ Used Up

Care ....

Notes ....

SWATCH

Swatch Name ....

Fabric Type ....

Designer ....

Content .... Colour ....

Length .... Width ....

Purchased From ....

Cost Price .... ☐ Prewashed

Used ....

.... ☐ Used Up

Care ....

Notes ....

SWATCH

Swatch Name ....

Fabric Type ....

Designer ....

Content .... Colour ....

Length .... Width ....

Purchased From ....

Cost Price .... ☐ Prewashed

Used ....

.... ☐ Used Up

Care ....

Notes ....

SWATCH

SWATCH

Swatch Name ....
Fabric Type ....
Designer ....
Content .... Colour ....
Length .... Width ....
Purchased From ....
Cost Price .... ☐ Prewashed
Used ....
.... ☐ Used Up
Care ....
Notes ....

SWATCH

Swatch Name ....
Fabric Type ....
Designer ....
Content .... Colour ....
Length .... Width ....
Purchased From ....
Cost Price .... ☐ Prewashed
Used ....
.... ☐ Used Up
Care ....
Notes ....

SWATCH

Swatch Name ....
Fabric Type ....
Designer ....
Content .... Colour ....
Length .... Width ....
Purchased From ....
Cost Price .... ☐ Prewashed
Used ....
.... ☐ Used Up
Care ....
Notes ....

Swatch Name ....

Fabric Type ....

Designer ....

Content .... Colour ....

Length .... Width ....

Purchased From ....

Cost Price .... □ Prewashed

Used ....

.... □ Used Up

Care ....

Notes ....

SWATCH

Swatch Name ....

Fabric Type ....

Designer ....

Content .... Colour ....

Length .... Width ....

Purchased From ....

Cost Price .... □ Prewashed

Used ....

.... □ Used Up

Care ....

Notes ....

SWATCH

Swatch Name ....

Fabric Type ....

Designer ....

Content .... Colour ....

Length .... Width ....

Purchased From ....

Cost Price .... □ Prewashed

Used ....

.... □ Used Up

Care ....

Notes ....

SWATCH

SWATCH

Swatch Name ....

Fabric Type ....

Designer ....

Content .... Colour ....

Length .... Width ....

Purchased From ....

Cost Price .... ☐ Prewashed

Used ....

.... ☐ Used Up

Care ....

Notes ....

SWATCH

Swatch Name ....

Fabric Type ....

Designer ....

Content .... Colour ....

Length .... Width ....

Purchased From ....

Cost Price .... ☐ Prewashed

Used ....

.... ☐ Used Up

Care ....

Notes ....

SWATCH

Swatch Name ....

Fabric Type ....

Designer ....

Content .... Colour ....

Length .... Width ....

Purchased From ....

Cost Price .... ☐ Prewashed

Used ....

.... ☐ Used Up

Care ....

Notes ....

Swatch Name ....

Fabric Type ....

Designer ....

Content .... Colour ....

Length .... Width ....

Purchased From ....

Cost Price .... □ Prewashed

Used ....

.... □ Used Up

Care ....

Notes ....

SWATCH

Swatch Name ....

Fabric Type ....

Designer ....

Content .... Colour ....

Length .... Width ....

Purchased From ....

Cost Price .... □ Prewashed

Used ....

.... □ Used Up

Care ....

Notes ....

SWATCH

Swatch Name ....

Fabric Type ....

Designer ....

Content .... Colour ....

Length .... Width ....

Purchased From ....

Cost Price .... □ Prewashed

Used ....

.... □ Used Up

Care ....

Notes ....

SWATCH

SWATCH	Swatch Name ....
	Fabric Type ....
	Designer ....
	Content .... Colour ....
	Length .... Width ....
	Purchased From ....
	Cost Price .... ☐ Prewashed
	Used ....
	.... ☐ Used Up
	Care ....
	Notes ....

SWATCH	Swatch Name ....
	Fabric Type ....
	Designer ....
	Content .... Colour ....
	Length .... Width ....
	Purchased From ....
	Cost Price .... ☐ Prewashed
	Used ....
	.... ☐ Used Up
	Care ....
	Notes ....

SWATCH	Swatch Name ....
	Fabric Type ....
	Designer ....
	Content .... Colour ....
	Length .... Width ....
	Purchased From ....
	Cost Price .... ☐ Prewashed
	Used ....
	.... ☐ Used Up
	Care ....
	Notes ....

Swatch Name ....

Fabric Type ....

Designer ....

Content .... Colour ....

Length .... Width ....

Purchased From ....

Cost Price .... □ Prewashed

Used ....

.... □ Used Up

Care ....

Notes ....

SWATCH

Swatch Name ....

Fabric Type ....

Designer ....

Content .... Colour ....

Length .... Width ....

Purchased From ....

Cost Price .... □ Prewashed

Used ....

.... □ Used Up

Care ....

Notes ....

SWATCH

Swatch Name ....

Fabric Type ....

Designer ....

Content .... Colour ....

Length .... Width ....

Purchased From ....

Cost Price .... □ Prewashed

Used ....

.... □ Used Up

Care ....

Notes ....

SWATCH

SWATCH

Swatch Name ....
Fabric Type ....
Designer ....
Content .... Colour ....
Length .... Width ....
Purchased From ....
Cost Price .... ☐ Prewashed
Used ....
.... ☐ Used Up
Care ....
Notes ....

SWATCH

Swatch Name ....
Fabric Type ....
Designer ....
Content .... Colour ....
Length .... Width ....
Purchased From ....
Cost Price .... ☐ Prewashed
Used ....
.... ☐ Used Up
Care ....
Notes ....

SWATCH

Swatch Name ....
Fabric Type ....
Designer ....
Content .... Colour ....
Length .... Width ....
Purchased From ....
Cost Price .... ☐ Prewashed
Used ....
.... ☐ Used Up
Care ....
Notes ....

Swatch Name ....

Fabric Type ....

Designer ....

Content .... Colour ....

Length .... Width ....

Purchased From ....

Cost Price .... □ Prewashed

Used ....

.... □ Used Up

Care ....

Notes ....

SWATCH

Swatch Name ....

Fabric Type ....

Designer ....

Content .... Colour ....

Length .... Width ....

Purchased From ....

Cost Price .... □ Prewashed

Used ....

.... □ Used Up

Care ....

Notes ....

SWATCH

Swatch Name ....

Fabric Type ....

Designer ....

Content .... Colour ....

Length .... Width ....

Purchased From ....

Cost Price .... □ Prewashed

Used ....

.... □ Used Up

Care ....

Notes ....

SWATCH

SWATCH

Swatch Name ....
Fabric Type ....
Designer ....
Content .... Colour ....
Length .... Width ....
Purchased From ....
Cost Price .... ☐ Prewashed
Used ....
.... ☐ Used Up
Care ....
Notes ....

SWATCH

Swatch Name ....
Fabric Type ....
Designer ....
Content .... Colour ....
Length .... Width ....
Purchased From ....
Cost Price .... ☐ Prewashed
Used ....
.... ☐ Used Up
Care ....
Notes ....

SWATCH

Swatch Name ....
Fabric Type ....
Designer ....
Content .... Colour ....
Length .... Width ....
Purchased From ....
Cost Price .... ☐ Prewashed
Used ....
.... ☐ Used Up
Care ....
Notes ....

Swatch Name ....

Fabric Type ....

Designer ....

Content .... Colour ....

Length .... Width ....

Purchased From ....

Cost Price .... □ Prewashed

Used ....

.... □ Used Up

Care ....

Notes ....

SWATCH

Swatch Name ....

Fabric Type ....

Designer ....

Content .... Colour ....

Length .... Width ....

Purchased From ....

Cost Price .... □ Prewashed

Used ....

.... □ Used Up

Care ....

Notes ....

SWATCH

Swatch Name ....

Fabric Type ....

Designer ....

Content .... Colour ....

Length .... Width ....

Purchased From ....

Cost Price .... □ Prewashed

Used ....

.... □ Used Up

Care ....

Notes ....

SWATCH

SWATCH

Swatch Name ....
Fabric Type ....
Designer ....
Content .... Colour ....
Length .... Width ....
Purchased From ....
Cost Price .... ☐ Prewashed
Used ....
.... ☐ Used Up
Care ....
Notes ....

SWATCH

Swatch Name ....
Fabric Type ....
Designer ....
Content .... Colour ....
Length .... Width ....
Purchased From ....
Cost Price .... ☐ Prewashed
Used ....
.... ☐ Used Up
Care ....
Notes ....

SWATCH

Swatch Name ....
Fabric Type ....
Designer ....
Content .... Colour ....
Length .... Width ....
Purchased From ....
Cost Price .... ☐ Prewashed
Used ....
.... ☐ Used Up
Care ....
Notes ....

Swatch Name	....
Fabric Type	....
Designer	....
Content	.... Colour ....
Length	.... Width ....
Purchased From	....
Cost Price	.... □ Prewashed
Used	....
	.... □ Used Up
Care	....
Notes	....

SWATCH

Swatch Name	....
Fabric Type	....
Designer	....
Content	.... Colour ....
Length	.... Width ....
Purchased From	....
Cost Price	.... □ Prewashed
Used	....
	.... □ Used Up
Care	....
Notes	....

SWATCH

Swatch Name	....
Fabric Type	....
Designer	....
Content	.... Colour ....
Length	.... Width ....
Purchased From	....
Cost Price	.... □ Prewashed
Used	....
	.... □ Used Up
Care	....
Notes	....

SWATCH

SWATCH

Swatch Name ....
Fabric Type ....
Designer ....
Content .... Colour ....
Length .... Width ....
Purchased From ....
Cost Price .... ☐ Prewashed
Used ....
.... ☐ Used Up
Care ....
Notes ....

SWATCH

Swatch Name ....
Fabric Type ....
Designer ....
Content .... Colour ....
Length .... Width ....
Purchased From ....
Cost Price .... ☐ Prewashed
Used ....
.... ☐ Used Up
Care ....
Notes ....

SWATCH

Swatch Name ....
Fabric Type ....
Designer ....
Content .... Colour ....
Length .... Width ....
Purchased From ....
Cost Price .... ☐ Prewashed
Used ....
.... ☐ Used Up
Care ....
Notes ....

Swatch Name	
Fabric Type	
Designer	
Content .... Colour	
Length .... Width	SWATCH
Purchased From	
Cost Price .... □ Prewashed	
Used	
.... □ Used Up	
Care	
Notes	

Swatch Name	
Fabric Type	
Designer	
Content .... Colour	
Length .... Width	SWATCH
Purchased From	
Cost Price .... □ Prewashed	
Used	
.... □ Used Up	
Care	
Notes	

Swatch Name	
Fabric Type	
Designer	
Content .... Colour	
Length .... Width	SWATCH
Purchased From	
Cost Price .... □ Prewashed	
Used	
.... □ Used Up	
Care	
Notes	

SWATCH	Swatch Name ....
	Fabric Type ....
	Designer ....
	Content .... Colour ....
	Length .... Width ....
	Purchased From ....
	Cost Price .... ☐ Prewashed
	Used ....
	.... ☐ Used Up
	Care ....
	Notes ....

SWATCH	Swatch Name ....
	Fabric Type ....
	Designer ....
	Content .... Colour ....
	Length .... Width ....
	Purchased From ....
	Cost Price .... ☐ Prewashed
	Used ....
	.... ☐ Used Up
	Care ....
	Notes ....

SWATCH	Swatch Name ....
	Fabric Type ....
	Designer ....
	Content .... Colour ....
	Length .... Width ....
	Purchased From ....
	Cost Price .... ☐ Prewashed
	Used ....
	.... ☐ Used Up
	Care ....
	Notes ....

Swatch 1

Swatch Name ....

Fabric Type ....

Designer ....

Content .... Colour ....

Length .... Width ....

Purchased From ....

Cost Price .... ☐ Prewashed

Used ....

.... ☐ Used Up

Care ....

Notes ....

SWATCH

Swatch 2

Swatch Name ....

Fabric Type ....

Designer ....

Content .... Colour ....

Length .... Width ....

Purchased From ....

Cost Price .... ☐ Prewashed

Used ....

.... ☐ Used Up

Care ....

Notes ....

SWATCH

Swatch 3

Swatch Name ....

Fabric Type ....

Designer ....

Content .... Colour ....

Length .... Width ....

Purchased From ....

Cost Price .... ☐ Prewashed

Used ....

.... ☐ Used Up

Care ....

Notes ....

SWATCH

	Swatch Name ....
	Fabric Type ....
	Designer ....
	Content .... Colour ....
SWATCH	Length .... Width ....
	Purchased From ....
	Cost Price .... ☐ Prewashed
	Used ....
	.... ☐ Used Up
	Care ....
	Notes ....

	Swatch Name ....
	Fabric Type ....
	Designer ....
	Content .... Colour ....
SWATCH	Length .... Width ....
	Purchased From ....
	Cost Price .... ☐ Prewashed
	Used ....
	.... ☐ Used Up
	Care ....
	Notes ....

	Swatch Name ....
	Fabric Type ....
	Designer ....
	Content .... Colour ....
SWATCH	Length .... Width ....
	Purchased From ....
	Cost Price .... ☐ Prewashed
	Used ....
	.... ☐ Used Up
	Care ....
	Notes ....

Swatch Name ....

Fabric Type ....

Designer ....

Content .... Colour ....

Length .... Width ....

Purchased From ....

Cost Price .... □ Prewashed

Used ....

.... □ Used Up

Care ....

Notes ....

SWATCH

Swatch Name ....

Fabric Type ....

Designer ....

Content .... Colour ....

Length .... Width ....

Purchased From ....

Cost Price .... □ Prewashed

Used ....

.... □ Used Up

Care ....

Notes ....

SWATCH

Swatch Name ....

Fabric Type ....

Designer ....

Content .... Colour ....

Length .... Width ....

Purchased From ....

Cost Price .... □ Prewashed

Used ....

.... □ Used Up

Care ....

Notes ....

SWATCH

SWATCH

Swatch Name ....
Fabric Type ....
Designer ....
Content .... Colour ....
Length .... Width ....
Purchased From ....
Cost Price ....□ Prewashed
Used ....
....□ Used Up
Care ....
Notes ....

SWATCH

Swatch Name ....
Fabric Type ....
Designer ....
Content .... Colour ....
Length .... Width ....
Purchased From ....
Cost Price ....□ Prewashed
Used ....
....□ Used Up
Care ....
Notes ....

SWATCH

Swatch Name ....
Fabric Type ....
Designer ....
Content .... Colour ....
Length .... Width ....
Purchased From ....
Cost Price ....□ Prewashed
Used ....
....□ Used Up
Care ....
Notes ....

Swatch Name ....

Fabric Type ....

Designer ....

Content .... Colour ....

Length .... Width ....

Purchased From ....

Cost Price .... □ Prewashed

Used ....

.... □ Used Up

Care ....

Notes ....

SWATCH

Swatch Name ....

Fabric Type ....

Designer ....

Content .... Colour ....

Length .... Width ....

Purchased From ....

Cost Price .... □ Prewashed

Used ....

.... □ Used Up

Care ....

Notes ....

SWATCH

Swatch Name ....

Fabric Type ....

Designer ....

Content .... Colour ....

Length .... Width ....

Purchased From ....

Cost Price .... □ Prewashed

Used ....

.... □ Used Up

Care ....

Notes ....

SWATCH

SWATCH	Swatch Name .... Fabric Type .... Designer .... Content .... Colour .... Length .... Width .... Purchased From .... Cost Price .... ☐ Prewashed Used .... ☐ Used Up Care .... Notes ....

SWATCH	Swatch Name .... Fabric Type .... Designer .... Content .... Colour .... Length .... Width .... Purchased From .... Cost Price .... ☐ Prewashed Used .... ☐ Used Up Care .... Notes ....

SWATCH	Swatch Name .... Fabric Type .... Designer .... Content .... Colour .... Length .... Width .... Purchased From .... Cost Price .... ☐ Prewashed Used .... ☐ Used Up Care .... Notes ....

Swatch Name ....

Fabric Type ....

Designer ....

Content .... Colour ....

Length .... Width ....

Purchased From ....

Cost Price .... □ Prewashed

Used ....

.... □ Used Up

Care ....

Notes ....

SWATCH

Swatch Name ....

Fabric Type ....

Designer ....

Content .... Colour ....

Length .... Width ....

Purchased From ....

Cost Price .... □ Prewashed

Used ....

.... □ Used Up

Care ....

Notes ....

SWATCH

Swatch Name ....

Fabric Type ....

Designer ....

Content .... Colour ....

Length .... Width ....

Purchased From ....

Cost Price .... □ Prewashed

Used ....

.... □ Used Up

Care ....

Notes ....

SWATCH

SWATCH	Swatch Name .... Fabric Type .... Designer .... Content .... Colour .... Length .... Width .... Purchased From .... Cost Price .... □ Prewashed Used .... □ Used Up Care .... Notes ....
SWATCH	Swatch Name .... Fabric Type .... Designer .... Content .... Colour .... Length .... Width .... Purchased From .... Cost Price .... □ Prewashed Used .... □ Used Up Care .... Notes ....
SWATCH	Swatch Name .... Fabric Type .... Designer .... Content .... Colour .... Length .... Width .... Purchased From .... Cost Price .... □ Prewashed Used .... □ Used Up Care .... Notes ....

Swatch Name	
Fabric Type	
Designer	
Content .... Colour	SWATCH
Length .... Width	
Purchased From	
Cost Price .... □ Prewashed	
Used	
.... □ Used Up	
Care	
Notes	

Swatch Name	
Fabric Type	
Designer	
Content .... Colour	SWATCH
Length .... Width	
Purchased From	
Cost Price .... □ Prewashed	
Used	
.... □ Used Up	
Care	
Notes	

Swatch Name	
Fabric Type	
Designer	
Content .... Colour	SWATCH
Length .... Width	
Purchased From	
Cost Price .... □ Prewashed	
Used	
.... □ Used Up	
Care	
Notes	

SWATCH

Swatch Name ....
Fabric Type ....
Designer ....
Content .... Colour ....
Length .... Width ....
Purchased From ....
Cost Price .... ☐ Prewashed
Used ....
.... ☐ Used Up
Care ....
Notes ....

SWATCH

Swatch Name ....
Fabric Type ....
Designer ....
Content .... Colour ....
Length .... Width ....
Purchased From ....
Cost Price .... ☐ Prewashed
Used ....
.... ☐ Used Up
Care ....
Notes ....

SWATCH

Swatch Name ....
Fabric Type ....
Designer ....
Content .... Colour ....
Length .... Width ....
Purchased From ....
Cost Price .... ☐ Prewashed
Used ....
.... ☐ Used Up
Care ....
Notes ....

Swatch Name ....

Fabric Type ....

Designer ....

Content .... Colour ....

Length .... Width ....

Purchased From ....

Cost Price .... □ Prewashed

Used ....

.... □ Used Up

Care ....

Notes ....

SWATCH

Swatch Name ....

Fabric Type ....

Designer ....

Content .... Colour ....

Length .... Width ....

Purchased From ....

Cost Price .... □ Prewashed

Used ....

.... □ Used Up

Care ....

Notes ....

SWATCH

Swatch Name ....

Fabric Type ....

Designer ....

Content .... Colour ....

Length .... Width ....

Purchased From ....

Cost Price .... □ Prewashed

Used ....

.... □ Used Up

Care ....

Notes ....

SWATCH

SWATCH

Swatch Name ....
Fabric Type ....
Designer ....
Content .... Colour ....
Length .... Width ....
Purchased From ....
Cost Price .... □ Prewashed
Used ....
.... □ Used Up
Care ....
Notes ....

SWATCH

Swatch Name ....
Fabric Type ....
Designer ....
Content .... Colour ....
Length .... Width ....
Purchased From ....
Cost Price .... □ Prewashed
Used ....
.... □ Used Up
Care ....
Notes ....

SWATCH

Swatch Name ....
Fabric Type ....
Designer ....
Content .... Colour ....
Length .... Width ....
Purchased From ....
Cost Price .... □ Prewashed
Used ....
.... □ Used Up
Care ....
Notes ....

Printed in Great Britain
by Amazon